INSTRUCTIONS
to the
DOUBLE

INSTRUCTIONS TO THE DOUBLE

POEMS BY TESS GALLAGHER

CARNEGIE MELLON UNIVERSITY PRESS
PITTSBURGH 1994

Library of Congress Catalog Card Number: 94-70468
ISBN 0-88748-202-3
Copyright© 1976 by Tess Gallagher
All rights reserved
Printed and bound in the United States of America

First Carnegie Mellon University Press Edition, June 1994

ACKNOWLEDGEMENTS:
Some of these poems first appeared in the following
anthologies and periodicals:
*Antaeus, Poetry Northwest, The Saturday Review, American
Poetry Review* (selections by Stanley Kunitz), *Anthology of
National Academy of American Poets Award Winners 1970-
1973, Mundus Artium* (International Womens' Issue),
*Montana Gothic, Borestone Mountain Best Poems of 1973,
Antioch Review, Fiction International, Tractor: Sympathy &
Coincidence, St. Lawrence Sea-way Valley Anthology, The
Iowa Review, The American Poetry Anthology, Back Door.*
'Coming Home,' 'Breasts,' 'Zero' and 'Snowheart' appeared
originally in *The New Yorker.*

Some of these poems were included in *Stepping Outside,*
a limited edition published by The Penumbra Press,
Lisbon, Iowa, 1974.

Epigraphs are from the following sources—
Ten Sonnets to Orpheus by R.M. Rilke, trans. by Robert Bly
(Mudra Press). Copyright © 1975 Robert Bly.
Discovery of the Square by Bruno Munari (George Wittenborn
Co.). Copyright © 1973 Bruno Munari.
The Ethics of Ambiguity by Simone de Beauvoir, trans. by
Bernard Frechtman (Citadel Press). Copyright © 1948 by
Philosophical Library.
The Diary of Anaïs Nin, v. 2 (Harcourt Brace & World).
Copyright © 1967 Anaïs Nin.
Richard Shelton's lines are from his poem 'Last Time,' first
published in *American Poetry Review.*
C.P. Cavafy Collected Poems trans. by Edmund Keeley and
Philip Sherrard, edited by George Savadis. Copyright © 1975
by Princeton University Press. Reprinted by permission of
Princeton University Press.
The Voice of Things by Francis Ponge, trans. by Beth Archer
(McGraw-Hill). Copyright © 1974 Editions Gallimard.

CONTENTS

for my sister, Stevie

"Even though images in the pool
seem so blurry:
grasp the main thing.

Only in the double kingdom, there
alone, do voices become
undying and tender."
                    —Rainer Maria Rilke
                    (tr. by Robert Bly)

I

"A woman suffering from a brain damage
disease was incapable of copying a square.
...When asked what these figures might mean
she replied, 'The windows of a church.' She
did not draw squares without significance."
—Bruno Munari

Kidnaper

He motions me over with a question.
He is lost. I believe him. It seems
he calls my name. I move
closer. He says it again, the name
of someone he loves. I step back pretending

not to hear. I suspect
the street he wants
does not exist, but I am glad to point
away from myself. While he turns
I slip off my wristwatch, already laying a trail
for those who must find me
tumbled like an abandoned car
into the ravine. I lie

without breath for days among ferns.
Pine needles drift
onto my face and breasts
like the tiny hands
of watches. Cars pass.
I imagine it's him
coming back. My death
is not needed. The sun climbs again
for everyone. He lifts me
like a bride

and the leaves fall from my shoulders
in twenty-dollar bills.
"You must have been cold," he says
covering me with his handkerchief.
"You must have given me up."

A Poem in Translation

After years smuggling poems
out of an unknown country
you have been discovered by a known
and skillful master. Your language
is foreign and eligible, your circumstances
Russian, complete with prison camps
and midnight journeys by train
through the Urals. Someone is always taking
your hand as a stranger, entrusting you
with a few saved belongings
before he is led away.

You too are led, a pair of eyes
wearing sight like an armor.
You witness it all. You do not suffer
the physical shame, your clothes
taken from you, your body
made to stand with the weeping others.
Somehow you are not harmed.
You stitch a cry into the hem of your coat
to be unraveled in a land of comfort.

They work over the lines like a corpse
taken from the ground. Gradually
they heap their own flesh
over what has remained,
the beautiful gaps and silences.

In the new language you are awkward.
You don't agree with yourself,
these versions of what you *meant*
to say. Like a journalist, one has written
"throat" where you have said
"throat." Another uses his ears
as a mouth; he writes like an orator
in a bathroom, not "tears"
but "sobbing."

Still another has only heard your name
and the title of one poem
full of proper names, rivers
and cities no one bothers
to translate. All his poems begin here
and move into the dream of you
as the ideal sacrifice, redeeming him
from a language he knows too well
to say anything simply.

One night (it always happens at night)
these translations, against all precautions,
are smuggled back to you by a woman
looking much like yourself. She
takes your hand and leads you away
into a room where each one calls you
by his name and you enter the solitary
kingdom of your face.

Breasts

14

The day you came
this world got its hold on me.
Summer grass and the four of us pounding hell
out of each other for god knows what
green murder of the skull.
Swart nubbins, I noticed you then,
my mother shaking a gritty rag from the porch
to get my shirt on this minute. Brothers,
that was the parting of our ways, for then
you got me down by something else than flesh.
By the loose skin of a cotton shirt
you kept me to the ground
until the bloody gout hung in my face like a web.

Little mothers, I can't find your children.
I have looked in a man
who moved through the air like a god.
He brought me clouds
and the loose stars of his goings.
Another kissed me on a pier in Georgia
but there was blood on his hands,
bad whiskey in the wind. The last one,
he made me a liar until I stole
what I could not win. Loves,
what is this mirror you have left me in?

I could have told you at the start   15
there would be trouble
from other hands, how the sharp mouths
would find you where you slept.
But I have hurt you as certainly
with cold sorrowings as anyone,
have come the long way
over broken ground to this softness.
Good clowns, how could I know, all along
it was your blundering mercies kept me alive
when heaven was a luckless dream.

Coming Home

As usual, I was desperate.
I went through your house as if I owned it.
I said, "I need This, This and This."
But contrary to all I know of you,
you did not answer, only looked after me.

I've never seen the house so empty, mother.
Even the rugs felt it, how little
they covered. And what have you done
with the plants? How thankfully
we thought their green replaced us.

You were keeping something like a light.
I had seen it before, a place you'd never been
or never came back from. It was a special way
your eyes looked out over the water. Whitecaps
lifted the bay and you said, "He should be here
by now."

How he always came back; the drinking,
the fishing at night, all
the ruthless ships he unloaded.
That was the miracle of our lives. Even now
he won't stay out of what I have
to say to you.

But they worry me, those boxes 17
of clothes I left in your basement. Sometimes
I think of home as a storehouse, the more
we leave behind, the less
you say. The last time
I couldn't take anything.

So I'm always coming back like tonight,
in a temper, brushing the azaleas
on the doorstep. What did you mean
by it, this tenderness
that is a whip, a longing?

The Woman Who Raised Goats

Dear ones, in those days it was otherwise.
I was suited more to an obedience
of windows. If anyone had asked,
I would have said: "Windows are my prologue."

My father worked on the docks
in a cold little harbor, unhappily
dedicated to what was needed
by the next and further
harbors. My brothers
succeeded him in this, but when I,
in that town's forsaken luster, offered myself,
the old men in the hiring hall creeled
back in their chairs, fanning themselves
with their cards, with their gloves.
"Saucey," they said. "She's saucey!"

Denial, O my Senators,
takes a random shape. The matter
drove me to wearing
a fedora. Soon, the gowns, the amiable
forgeries: a powdery sailor, the blue silk
pillow given by a great aunt, my name
embroidered on it like a ship, the stitched
horse too, with its red plume and its bird eyes
glowing, glowing. There was the education
of my "sensibilities."

All this is nothing to you.   19
You have eaten my only dress, and the town
drifts every day now
toward the harbor. But always,
above the town, above
the harbor, there is the town,
the harbor, the caves and hollows
when the cargo of lights
is gone.

Cows, a Vision

20

Some monster bird, the barn
flings its shadow across the field
to the walnut grove. The cows
with milk-worn bodies muffle
its cry, the cry of riverbeds
gone white. In the rafters
the wings of swallows breathe
over eggs like eyes. If the sun
falls on them they must open
and fly. I was born that way,
some beak of light lifting a straw.

The cows were never born. They came
with the land, with the bucket
hanging in the well, with the iron
bed and the empty cat who slept
by the clock and ticked only
to your hand. You took it all
because it was the cat's dream
or the clock's or the empty bed
waiting. You filled everything,
the barn, the bucket, the bed,
even the empty dream and then
you built yourself a front porch
where, of an evening, you could
sit down to bullfrogs and rusty owls.

It was up to the cows after that
to keep things going. Their mouths
were always faithful, turning
like windmills the heavy heart
of the moon. For a moment toward dawn
or dusk the cows pause in their work
and a secret moon swells in them,
threatens to carry them over the barn
and away. When we die, I tell you,
that moon will find its stars and nothing
will keep them down. You aren't worried.
For you there is only more good land.

Black Money

His lungs heaving all day in a sulphur mist,
then dusk, the lunch pail torn from him
before he reaches the house, his children
a cloud of swallows about him.
At the stove in the tumbled rooms, the wife,
her back the wall he fights most, and she
with no weapon but silence
and to keep him from the bed.

In their sleep the mill hums and turns
at the edge of water. Blue smoke
swells the night and they drift
from the graves they have made for each other,
float out from the open-mouthed sleep
of their children, past banks and businesses,
the used car lots, liquor store, the swings in the park.

The mill burns on, now a burst of cinders,
now whistles screaming down the bay, saws jagged
in half light. Then like a whip
the sun across the bed, windows high with mountains
and the sleepers fallen to pillows
as gulls fall, tilting
against their shadows on the log booms.
Again the trucks shudder the wood framed houses
passing to the mill. My father
snorts, splashes in the bathroom,

throws open our doors to cowboy music
on the radio, hearts are cheating,
somebody is alone, there's blood in Tulsa.
Out the back yard the night-shift men rattle
the gravel in the alley going home.
My father fits goggles to his head.

From his pocket he takes anything metal,
the pearl-handled jack knife, a ring of keys,
and for us, black money shoveled
from the sulphur pyramids heaped in the distance
like yellow gold. Coffee bottle tucked in his armpit
he swaggers past the chicken coop,
a pack of cards at his breast.
In a fan of light beyond him
the Kino Maru pulls out for Seattle,
some black star climbing
the deep globe of his eye.

Even Now You Are Leaving

Not to let ourselves know
by a hand held too long, as this last,
words no part of any other, like a mule
trained to carry anything
and not mean it. Just so these lips
puffed from where you ran into yourself
in a car the night before, the wheel
turning through your mouth
like something you might have said.

I can't believe your face, that
it could fall from here, let alone
my own. Yet you prove it, the chin
large now as a forehead. Some nearness
has done this to you, or the lack
of it. That scheme you had
for making us rich, I want to tell you
it worked, though Alaska
stayed due north
and you never touched.

The spar tree ax
swings from a tree you rigged
to hold that clearing. I can't look up.
The tree's too white
and cedar an easy fire. Father,
some neglect is killing us all, but yours
has a name of its own: family,
something gone on without you, your eyes
ruined and terrible in a face
even now you are leaving.

The Coats

They made you complicated,
a new one each year
and underneath, the same
old print dress. Outside
under the maples you were smart
and garrulous on my grandfather's arm
walking down Valley Street
to the shops, talking into his silence
as into some idea of yourself
grown to your side.

Yet you loved telling how
you were engaged to another
the night he took you off
in his buckboard. Marriage too
came like an impulse
to turn against yourself. Life
caught you up in its clumsy arms
and danced you out of your Oklahoma
youth into the milltown
of my birth, you in your new coat,
leading me into the dimestore
to buy silk ribbons.

Shut in the closet, your coats
were a family of witnesses
who could not remember you.
They were waiting for the one
to send them all again
into the weather. Standing
before your mirror once
in the dark of the bedroom
I put myself into a heavy tweed
with its cold silk lining. The wide arms
were a hiding place; the hem
brushed my patent leather shoes.
It was a bargaining
that I should turn into the room,
your age about me like a sack.

I wanted to throw something over you
the day they carried you off
like a trophy in your silk lining.
Rosy and familiar you received each of us
in a housedress that denied you
were going anywhere. That year
the winter came over the ground
like a rich white pelt.
I thought of you accepting it,
something chosen, a comfort
that had sought you out
in the cold of the land.

II

"... for a being who, from the very start, would be an exact co-incidence with himself, in a perfect plentitude, the notion of having-to-be would have no meaning."
—Simone de Beauvoir

When You Speak to Me

Take care when you speak to me.
I might listen, I might
draw near as the flame
breathing with the log, breathing
with the tree it has not
forgotten. I might
put my face
next to
your face
in your nameless trouble,
in your trouble
and name.

It is a thing I learned
without learning; a hand
is a stronger mouth, a kiss could
crack the skull, these
words, small steps
in the air calling
the secret hands, the mouths
hidden in the flesh.

32

This isn't robbery.
This isn't your blood for my
tears, no confidence
in trade or barter. I may
say nothing back
which is to hear
after you the fever
inside the words we say
apart, the words we say so hard
they fall apart.

Two Stories

[To the author of a story taken
from the death of my uncle, Porter
Morris, killed June 7, 1972.]

You kept the names, the flies
of who they were, mine
gone carnival, ugly Tessie.
It got wilder but nothing
personal. The plot had me
an easy lay for a buck.
My uncle came to life
as my lover. At 16
the murderer stabbed cows
and mutilated chickens. Grown,
you gave him a crowbar that happened
to be handy twice. Then you made him
do it alone. For me
it took three drunks, a gun, the house
on fire. There was a black space
between trees where I told you.

The shape of my uncle
spread its arms on the wire springs
in the yard and the neighbors
came to look at his shadow
caught there under the nose
of his dog. They left that angel

34 to you. Your killer never
mentioned money. Like us he wanted
to outlive his hand in the sure blood
of another. The veins of my uncle streaked
where the house had been. They watched
until morning. Your man found a faucet
in an old man's side. His pants
were stiff with it for days. He left
the crowbar on Tessie's porch like a bone.

My weapon was never found.
The murderers drove a white
stationwagon and puked
as they went. They hoped
for 100 dollar bills stuffed
in a lard can. But a farmer
keeps his money in cattle
and land. They threw his billfold
into the ditch like an empty
bird. One ran away. Two stayed
with women. I kept the news
blind. You took it from my mouth,
shaped it for the market, still
a dream worse than I remembered.

Now there is the story of me
reading your story and the one
of you saying it
doesn't deserve such care.
I say it matters
that the dog stays by the chimney
for months, and a rain
soft as the sleep of cats
enters the land, emptied
of its cows, its wire gates pulled down
by hands that never dug
the single well, this whitened field.

36

I don't know any beautiful words
but a pile of rocks
you set up like a city
at Dungeness where the crabs
crawl up to make fists
at the water. I did that, you said,
and we walked on down the beach, me
after stones smooth enough to remember
all those nights in waves and stars.

There was a place you took me once
instead of a room, so much wind
we couldn't stand and my print dress
full of willows flying into
our faces. To be buried in Plains,
Montana, near the town in the postmark:
Paradise.

The turtle's heart. If we speak of it,
it crawls from its sky of bone, goes
walking, open, furious with light,
brushing the ground with its hidden beak.

Over it the sky is one huge breath
we have already died of.

The Absence

I am writing this out of vengeance
which is a hurt given to the self
in the name of another. It has to do
with becoming a purpose
which is an absence not unlike
a gun. A man fired one
into an ocean in back of my house.
It was an act of bravery. The birds
went free because it was my
back porch and an ocean
behind it. He knew a target
when he saw one, those fists loose
in his eye. That is the way of targets,
one as good as another until
you decide. The ocean was there
and a recognition of the gun
for the ocean and the need too
of the man to leave himself out
which is a way of beginning
again. I am writing this
out of vengeance and the word
because has nothing to do
with it. The reason forgets
itself. The man has fired.

38   The gun and the ocean. What
did you mean? The man
and the ocean. The gun
has fired. The ocean is becoming
a purpose I can say and we
are becoming more than the gun,
this water emptying
without a sign.

Snowheart

In our houses, the snow keeps us
traveling. It says: your life
is where you are. The phone
all day ringing by itself
over the next lot, isn't for you.

The man with the perfect
haircut makes a track
across the lawn, holding
his books like a
breast. *Snowheart*

you have said: *don't cut your black hair.*

Love's the only debt.
He's up again
and riding the best mare
ten miles by moonlight, the
spruce-backed fiddle
under his arm.

"Dance us the next one too.
If day comes, don't
tell. Let the horse
go home alone."

Snowheart. Someone's horse
circles the near house.
There is snow
on its back.

The Perfect Sky

40

It is too easy
to speak of the lovers,
their crimson hands, the many lips
that may not touch
without a moon between.

It is too easy to call up
from the wordless hedge
the seal-colored birds, to fix them
a dark constellation
about the cloud
that even now is fading.

It is easy too
to see the woman in the doorway
and further, how she passes
to the familiar rooms
toward the slow faces,
how from her hands are falling
the endless, the wooden plates.

Cunningly, cunningly
she gives to those of her table
and they without apology
raise their bright forks, raise
and lower, fattening imperceptibly
in the yellowed light. Made calm
by some deeper neglect
her silhouette returns to the doorway.

The birds flown so recently from the hedge
reappear as do the lovers
of whom it has been easy
to speak. Finally, it is the missing cloud
that concerns us
and what we may say
before the perfect sky.

Secret

It wants to crow, flaps
but will not fly. It struts
in a circle, looks twice
in the same direction, steps forward
to be on the edge.
It cocks its head, listens
first to a tree in the distance,
then to itself. There is fur
at the corner of its eye.
A beak opens saying: "These feathers
will not make a bird. I am leaving
everything out. I am leaving you out."

The Horse in the Drugstore

wants to be admired.
He no longer thinks of what he has given up
to stand here, the milk-white reason
of chickens over his head in the night, the grass
spilling on through the day. No, it is enough
to stand so with his polished chest among the nipples
and bibs, the cotton and multiple sprays, with his
                                        black lips
parted just slightly and the forehooves doubled back
in the lavender air. He has learned here when
                                    maligned to snort
dimes and to carry the inscrutable bruise like a bride.

Cage

44

There were no tigers with us that night,
only the sad cats
lost in their tails.
What we said stayed in its chair.
There were hands again,
my hair a shade across your knees.

Yet we remember losing track of the crowd
in a murderous hour,
the failed shouts
sounding how far we had come from the trees,
from the dark pools by the roadside.

Now reason, the miserable bitch, circles
the spot we call
a trail, uses all we give,
will not be led by the tongue.
I make a promise; it becomes
a whip. I write a poem;
it believes in its cage.

Intimate as a fly it approaches.
On the platform a hand is lifted. Drums
slash tented air, the jaw
goes up like an ax. It enters.
It strides forward. It likes
to keep coming. Between us
a face turns back, yet it keeps on coming.

Strategy

I'll go; I'll say
forget that other, the one you took
to make the waiting shorter.
I'll say you didn't mean to
make a death of it like that
on the phone where the voice
is the head sent like a birth
before the body.

I'll put your head
on my woman's shoulders.
I'll walk all the way so she'll know
you meant it. You'll forgive her.
You'll give the last kiss
and when I walk you out of there,
you'll turn as you refuse to, you'll
turn, thinking it could start again
like the man who begs to stay
with his shadow.

If you look long enough
it will get too late. You'll both
turn into memories,
leaving no one to forget.
I won't listen. I'll
walk out of there.

The Discovery

for Robert Falcon Scott

46

Tonight I am eating my tracks
like the man who ate his dogs
coming before you to a singular
desolation. This moment I am all
intention, as it was with you
writing: "Had we lived," the blizzard,
the words locked in your hands.

So your blood was a stairway
when they found you with your men
huddled like dogs in the depths
of where you had lain. You were right
to make them come for you
with their sledges and dogs.
You had moved into yourselves
like some last extremity.

I could tell you
returning is only the memory
of something loved and denied.
We have met on the white plain,
the nightmare of sledges, buried
and live. Where were you going, wrapped
in your stoney arms, with your stumps
of feet going on like a thought
when the mind has gone out?

Croce e Delizia al Cor

Remember, and already the lapse in
vision pulls you back
too suddenly, the swing lowering
the boughs of the ash. You could sail forever
through the side of some fundamental right
you were giving yourself
at his expense.

The swing repeats the arc, the air
under you. Crouched
in a moving corner, this looking down
makes you feel specially weighted for falling,
an urge to get between assassinations
of either fixity, sky or ground.

Where you tempt the arc to be happy on its own,
the baby's buggy careens down cloudless skies
breaking your eyeglasses, both lenses at
once. So the frame presents the eyes
in a harmony not understood as the harbor
falls away through ships.

This necessity of returns
prolongs everything. The tree belongs to the
lawn, though the swing, it's true, is artificial,
heading like that over the girl in braids
eating a peanut butter sandwich near
the fence. She is inventing her turn
while the parents rub up against

48   our house in a paroxysm of bad advice. They
would praise the swing if it subdued
the tree. And yes, because you didn't look away,
something was settled.

Just then your mother steps out
of the lilac, meaning to leave you
with a last word. Call it a continuous hesitation,
her not wanting to admit pain which demands
credit and balance. "Anyone, afterall, can let things
go to hell," before the sun
smashes the horizon and you catch sight of the
buggy hurtling impossibly through an entire
generation of good intentions.

The harbor yawns in and
out. Behind, into branches, the nest
is a sky broken from you. It matches that holding
the ships just above water.
Even so, the baby will drown there on the lawn
with the broken lenses, the blur of intimate
conjunctions: that bird dying into the sweep of
your knees above the houses.

Zero

Stupid tranquility, to be most sure
in the abstract, the zebra
raising its head from the river, the clock
wound to the usual multitude, the junco bird
appearing as a miracle on the blind magician's
balcony. A thing among things,
the magician is there as an absolute, his
long sleeves, an attitude of sight
that amounts to seeing, the morning steady

in the orange grove. To sit with him
is to sense the luminous sides
of objects making a finite path
to an infinite doorway. See how he multiplies
himself like the doves in his hat
not flying away into the village
but resting in the white brocade
on the crook of his arm.

He walks the promenade, a procession
of explicit consequences, the funeral
climbing the hill with its tub
of roses. Magic powder clings
to his tongue, alum and ginger. A mild
contraction in the landscape, his reticence
to prove himself. Doesn't the sun

50   look as if it got there again
over the handkerchief snake
in his palm? This knot could make you cry,
how it slips past itself, now a
bracelet, now a white stem
drawn in the serious air of your breath,
letting itself down, the careful
ballerina closing the halo
of her partner's arms.

III

Songs of the Runaway Bride

"Put warm blankets on me because heat attracts me and makes me want to stay where I am. Turn on a strong warm voice. A strong voice which comes from the stomach also makes me want to stay on earth."

—Anaïs Nin

i

I saw him coming as light flows
over a roof through smoke.
His walk was a chain of ladders.
I thought I could come to the top
of what he saw, but the rungs
fell from my feet. So the air
makes a home of us.

All night the water muffled
the stair. Sleep ran like a fiber
through the streets.
I made ready for the bells
and the rooms anxious
to be fed, for the dynasty
of a limited memory, the polka,
the formal solution with an edge
of panic. Together and together—
the exact coffin of pleasure
crookedly in the blood.

ii

54   There are ceremonies even the dead regret.
        And your hand, which must be
        offered first. Regardless,
        there is an etiquette
        that accepts. We had been accepting
        a long time. I am a witness
        out of that persistence. The days
        were like that, standing
        and lost as you, the too serious girl
        locked in the yard.

iii

This travel backwards
stirs an opposite sleep,
the dream confessed to insure
my return. Your name
grows cruel in that clearing
near the bandstand. The lake
you built to resemble a heart
has new temptations, nets,
days repeating trees
you thought stood still.

Husband, all night I slept on your neck
and a man went through my dreams
and was not you. With a knife
I sliced the yellow dress
he mistook for me, until it was ribbons,
until it was rags. How did I come to this
crouching in sharpest grass?
I am deadly white. Painted floors
have struck your head. What I know
of it, your bloodshot eyes
from November to Christmas.

iv

56

I was glad they saw it, those
of his house, though I thought him
dead at first, doubled
on the lawn. His face.
I could have carried you alone
out of that openness.
There is grief also in things intended.
They saw you could not stand
from there, the sound of the grass,
how the difference had filled you
further than anyone could have
said, and we carried you,
like a room looking up,
into the house, into
its stairs.

Away from this I am wife
and another breathing.
My forehead as field
or cliff, the rain
a tin rushing outside
the window, so close,
your closed eyes, the bed
descending in a shaft of wideness
meant for me. Yet not to be sure
who it was you called, breaking
from words you came alone to,
but that: it was not me.

V

57

He was counting the cows. I watched
from a clump of scrub oak.
"Now," I thought, "we're even."
But the joy he took riding among them
while they tossed and ate
reached past me. His arm
gave blessing in their keeping. After me,
the house took in its leaves.

My grandfather's hat came floating
over the vines. I wore a ribbon
from the attic. The wagon
with its iron wheels struck the air
and I stood in the yard, opening
where the road passes like sleep
overheard, its stones sparking, the horses
falling away before the woods. My hand
waving, waving and the necks
of the black horses nodding in a milk of sunlight.

58   Ample cotton and over it
an apron, your crossing from barn
to house, the snow, the men
held near fences, near horses, the porch
not figuring in this, nor the well.
Your glare, grandmother, a shadowy pucker
below your hand in salute.
I approach by the side path, the rain barrel
and smokehouse, the solitary
chopping block. Above your work
some excess in the upper arms, a flapping
or myself enclosed, the glove-skin
of the squirrel pulled free between us, hot
and blue, steam flaring
even from the emptied fur.

Will you believe she gave in
for that? not the house fired
to a crust, nor its beds
aflame around the days of your childhood.
In the glow we saw the chimney
come mumbling towards us
through a stairway, its cats
ashes where the saddle
crashed. None of this. No,
nor Jacob, the portrait, burning after her,
the quilts stacked like cordwood
in the attic. Only for this, fan,
red fan, you gave your mother
and how she sat
rocking like an ocean, keeping the heat
going for the sake of the gift, to be
used, if not wanted, a sharpness
as though to say, "I am only waiting
to get out of this."

59

vii

60

Refinement, rule to be saluted and
robbed, how you dulled yourself
like a song scraped
on a stone. Soon the ships
did not know you. They whined
at their anchors below
the gulls in the harbor.

Not to call the fish
a scar to its water, but what comes
together in a single light.
Hands, lips, eyes
walk out of me. So the river
burns after us in a cry
that closes after trees, the banks
go dark.

The field thickens with stars.
It is a sign that again the land
has forgiven your hands.
Once I could speak under the dirt roof.
Today I bent on the gulf
of a dream. "Wild things sleep here,"
you said, and again the possum chased
by the best hound into the second chamber,
both sodden with breath, never to be
seen again. The boat set loose
on the lake with a provision
of fire. A horse shelters with me, or
how the light twitches on the hand-dug shelf.

viii

Mary, he calls me Mary   61
and I answer, though it is her name
unfolds the dead, my face
a pardon. "Your neck, so
like hers." All this a sleep.
None of these quilts has met
that hill or kneels again
in her, in me, little father, our kingly air.

62   I told you out of a dream
a train was rushing into a station
where everyone must get out.
At the last moment an overpowering
significance rescued the landscape.
Refusals, the alarms of the passengers.
When the station arrived
they had vanished
and the train went on
without them—a strange intensity.

We looked at the same place on a stone. 63
It was a habit we believed in.
All the time, the stone
had its own heart. All the time,
the earth was a sea
of stones. I saw myself
sailing; I saw myself
in the stone go sailing.

64

If absence deserves, as you say it
does, a voice which blinds itself
and recovers, let me complete
the assurance: a mouth pointing into
the water you cast like grain
into more water. Take
the ring from my hand: set it
on the table. In the next room
a tenderness we served together
rises from the fresh sheets.
There is more but it is bitter-sweet
and calls me back, leper-tongued
saying without arms
"*moja! moja!*" mine, oh mine.

IV

"We who care most,
who are most ruthless, go for the heart."
                    —Richard Shelton

"From all the things I did and all the
                    things I said
let no one try to find out who I was.
... Later, in a more perfect society,
someone else made just like me
is certain to appear and act freely..."
                    —C.P. Cavafy

Instructions to the Double

So now it's your turn, 67
little mother of silences, little
father of half-belief. Take up
this face, these daily rounds
with a cabbage under each arm
convincing the multitudes
that a well-made-anything
could save them. Take up
most of all, these hands
trained to an ornate piano
in a house on the other side
of the country.

I'm staying here
without music, without
applause. I'm not going
to wait up for you. Take
your time. Take mine
too. Get into some trouble
I'll have to account for. Walk
into some bars alone
with a slit in your skirt. Let
the men follow you on the street
with their clumsy propositions, their
loud hatreds of this and that. Keep
walking. Keep your head
up. They are calling to you—slut, mother,
virgin, whore, daughter, adultress, lover,
mistress, bitch, wife, cunt, harlot,
betrothed, Jezebel, Messalina, Diana,

Bethsheba, Rebecca, Lucretia, Mary,
Magdelena, Ruth, you—Niobe,
woman of the tombs.

Don't stop for anything, not
a caress or a promise. Go
to the temple of the poets, not
the one like a run-down country club,
but the one on fire
with so much it wants
to be done with. Say all the last words
and the first: hello, goodbye, yes,
I, no, please, always, never.

If anyone from the country club
asks if you write poems, say
your name is Lizzie Borden.
Show him your axe, the one
they gave you with a silver
blade, your name engraved there
like a whisper of their own.

If anyone calls you a witch,
burn for him; if anyone calls you
less or more than you are
let him burn for you.

It's a dangerous mission. You
could die out there. You
could live forever.

Stepping Outside

for Akhmatova

Hearing of you, I never lost a brother
though I have, never saw a husband to war,
though I have, never kept with my father
the emptiness of his hands, my mother
the dying of her womb.

Return: husbands, sons, fathers return.
Many with both arms, with dreams
broken in both eyes.
They try, they try
but they cannot tell us
what comes back with them.

One more has planted his hoe
in my heart like an ax, my farmer uncle
slain by thieves
in the night, burned down
with his house, buried, dug up
to prove he was no dog.
He was no dog.

You, who lived in your pain until it grew
its own face, would have left all this
like a monument in a field. Your words
would have made a feast of what ate you.

Sit with me.
No one has left; no one returns.

Beginning to Say No

is not to offer so much as a fist, is
to walk away firmly, as though
you had settled something foolish,
is to wear a tarantula in your buttonhole
yet smile invitingly, unmindful
how your own blood grows toward the irreversible
bite. No, I will not

go with you. No, that is not
alright. I'm not your sweet-dish, your
home-cooking, good looking daf-
fodil. Yes is no
reason to slay the cyclops. No
will not save it. And the cricket, "Yes, yes."

Fresh bait, fresh bait!
The search for the right hesitation
includes finally
unobstructed waters. Goodbye,
old happy-go-anyhow, old shoe
for any weather. Whose
candelabra are you? Whose
soft-guy, nevermind, nothing-to-lose ant hill?

"And," the despised connective,
is really an engine
until it is yes all day, until a light
is thrown against a wall
with some result. And
there is less doubt, yes or no,
for whatever you have been compelled to say
more than once.

The Loved One

Jealousies and the blue nights of the geese
infatuate the house, the scar
on the lover's pillow lifting the dream
through flesh. You were tearing out handfuls
of baby's breath, gypsophila
from under the window, the delicate weed

in the bridal bouquet. It meant to take you
with it, growing into the view of your father
looking ready to go off on a safari
in his short pants, carrying the paint can.
Secret orders from your mother, smoking
and playing solitaire on the patio.

The miniature garden near the fireplace
insinuates a hateful perpetual harmony
that makes you want to kick in
the side of the house, breaking like a madman
right through the plaster into your bedroom
frozen at 16 years. Loved one,

we know each other. Over our shoulders
you break the wishbone with yourself.
If this were all, we could pass from love
to reputation, say which hand cheats
the offering, which fear dismantles
this or that possibility. But you've

been there before us, ready to walk into the sea
in your sailor's cap, terrifying
the consequences of anyone's saying: Go ahead! go
ahead! and not looking back
as you take off your shirt.

Crossing

for Michael

74

I have looked at you
as one receives a letter mysteriously
over oceans, hands out of nowhere. And you
have looked back until the last possible moment
at the tulips brushing my throat, the wedding party
a nest of smiles behind us. Like applause
in a field, the summer lawn tilts away
and I have settled again on your arm,
a bird remembered for the sky it returns.

So much of what we come to
happens out of branches repeated
as the same water, reflections not broken
by the small blaze near a door, nor emptied
as faces taken first for their danger. And you
who have believed me, what I seem,
give all there is of pardon. Each resemblance,
each moon so like a moon, opens
on a river you cross always alone.
Yet we gather like a forest, the joys
that fall to us even in mockery, the usual world
of homes and lights, its true disguises.

Time Lapse with Tulips

That kiss meant to sear my heart forever—
it went right by.
And the way we walked out on Sundays
to the bakery like a very old couple, arm
on arm, that's gone too
though the street had a house with a harp
in the window.

Those tulips again.
They think if they keep being given away
by the black-haired man at our wedding
I will finally take them in time
for the photograph. But they are wrong.
This time I will hand them back or leave them
sitting in the mason jar
on the grass beside you.

See how the guests lean after me, their mouths
slightly open. Only now it's plain
they were never sure, that the picture
holding us all preserves
a symmetry of doubt with us
at the center, the pledge
of tulips red against my dress.

Whatever the picture says, it is wrong.
I take my image back, the white
petals that were standing a while at your side,
petals falling a while
at your side. Here instead,
the trick of flesh held again to your cheek.
Inside, the rare bone of my hand and that harp
seen through a window suddenly so tempting

you must rush into that closed room, you must
tear your fingers across it.

Perspectives in White

I come into your house
as one in a forest
comes to a cool sad moment
where all has been
stilled by the mercifully
not human. Covered, the furniture
keeps these shapes in sympathy,
the white chair a white cave
entering the hard glance of the wall.

The bedroom accepts a noxious
purity: white satin bedspread, mesh curtains,
frilled lamp on the bedstand, milkglass bottles
on the bureau. And the dreams
white too, so the rooms overlap,
so the mirrors join in a view missing
between windows, these messages
delivered and kept, speaking softly
as into a closet full of habitual
sunsets. The white voice
crosses itself with rewards
saying, "guests, guests, guests."

Complicity

The limbs are caught in each other
outside my window where the saw-men
have entered the tree. Dead limbs
pile up on the shadows.
Now a saw goes up on a rope
and the ground man steps back
for what falls. I tell him my father
rigged spar trees in the west.
I need a reason to watch
this tree come down.

He uses his weight on the rope
like a saw, then backs off.
The chainsaw snarls and jaws.
Over him, the tree and the wind: sawdust
over my house.

If a tree goes down among others
it makes its whole length felt
as something lost and final, not
this slow dispossession
of parts. I have heard a whole tree cry out
in the clearings my father made.
But this tree snaps and shudders
and calms itself back
into silence.

From the street, the houses
seem to have stepped away.

In my window the likeness
of the tree goes on, the light
opening and gathering
over my desk, over what I cannot heal.

The Likeness

> "One might say that stone,
> which does not regenerate,
> is in fact the only thing in nature
> that constantly dies."
>
> —Francis Ponge

To have felt much
in doubt of caring, is conviction enough
when a thing is done
and you tell me as in a story
how you sliced your breast
with a razor
not to let him go.

Now every man who sees you
by moonlight must kiss
that scar or scrape against it
in the night. And though you dismiss it
as proof against new love
they have seen your hand
go to it like a heart.

I could not show
where my own flesh closed
though the ridge is there
when I speak of it. A finger
traces a breath along the window
through the view, the river
which stays the same.

Each time the breath seems more
a part of the scene, a man
walks through it
and I am the same. You
open your blouse
to reflect the scar
and the man walks through it.

I am the same. I am always the same.

Corona

82 Personable shadow, you follow me into this
daylight-dream, the one even my body
knows nothing of.

This flesh is your halo, the meat you drag daily
across the earth like an injured
wife. The sun

surrounds us as the heart surrounds
the body. Let us
navigate each pleasure, each pain

like a doorway, its ambush: the mouth, the bouquet,
the six-story ladder, that
memory of a train

missed in Budapest, everything passing through.
The tail of a shirt
caresses the back of my brother who falls again

from the tractor in 1957. A woman's body
flies out of the house
like an insult. It is the day we are found

missing. See
the windows floating beside us into the next world,
admitting they don't know what they're for.

I will speak to you like a lover, not as one   83
I have used
to keep from being true. This water is a memory

of sleep, folding us
under. Your face
covers mine; the moon of your face blasted from a train

through faults of light in the trees—again and
again cut off, this water
taking up our hands.

The Calm

We were walking through the bees
and stars. Our mouths
made a sense without us.
I loved your hands
because of your mouth, each star
because of a life not chosen
by the hand. I told you,
don't say it, the loss
of our lives beyond us. You
said it. You said it
for the sake of a loneliness
together, for the praise of our eyes
going on without shadows.

Even now, when all our nights
have washed away
and the apples have left
the trees, I am keeping your place
where the high grass
has entered the song. Like a swarm
the heart moves with its separate
wings under the eaves.

If I knew where to find you
I would say goodbye
and have the hurtful ease of that,
but the gates are everywhere
and this calm—an imagined forgiveness,
the childhood before we meet again.

Rhododendrons

Like porches they trust their attachments,
or seem to, the road and the trees
leaving them open from both sides.
I have admired their spirit,
wild-headed women of the roadside,
how exclusion is only something glimpsed,
the locomotive dream that learns to go on
without caring for the landscape.

There is a spine in the soil
I have not praised enough:
its underhair of surface
clawed to the air. Elsewhere each shore
recommends an ease of boats, shoulders
nodding over salmon
who cross this sky with our faces.

I was justifying my confusion
the last time we walked this way.
I think I said some survivals need
a forest. But it was only the sound
of knowing. Assumptions
about roots put down like a deeper foot
seemed dangerous too.

These were flowers you did not cut,
iris and mums a kindness enough.
Some idea of relative dignities, I suppose,

86   let us spare each other; I came away
with your secret consent and this
lets you stand like a grief
telling itself over and over.

Even grief has instructions,
like the boats gathering light
from the water and the separate
extensions of the roots. So remembering
is only one more way of being alone
when the voice has gone everywhere
in the dusk of the porches
looking for the last thing to say.

NOTES

"Black Money": Sulphur, a pulp-mill by-product, turns silver black.

"February 17, 1975" is for Bill Gingery, suicide resulting from pressures arising during his term as head of Enforcement for the Civil Aeronautics Board.

"Snowheart" is dedicated to Rick Landry.

"*Croce e Delizia al Cor*": The title is from *La Traviata*, and translates, 'both the cross and the ecstacy of the heart.'

"Songs of the Runaway Bride": '*moja, moja*' in part xi is 'mine, mine,' taken from the Polish translation of James Joyce's *Finnegans Wake*.

Special thanks to Nelson Bentley, one of my first teachers. Also Margaret Matthieu and Esther Webster. Names which mean much to me: Larry Gallagher, Michelle Savelle, Francis McConnel, Michael Burkard, Laura Jensen.